WHA
Y~~OU FROM~~
WRITING
YOUR BOOK?

The Subtle Art Of Starting And Completing A Non-Fiction Book
(Or Even A Thesis) In 4 Simple Steps

MANEESH DUTT

Dedicated to the writer in
you,
who has been trying very
hard to take birth
but has'nt ...till now !

CONTENTS

INTRODUCTION

Of the many who have a desire to pen a book one day, there is a small number that actually start writing their book, and an even smaller percentage, who complete it. Irrespective of whether you are yet to start your manuscript or you have an incomplete one saved somewhere in your laptop, this Book provides a step by step easy method to bring your book to life. The essence of the method that I present in this Book aims at making the process of book writing extremely enjoyable so that it no longer appears a daunting task. It should never be one!

A quick look at my own story should convince you that if I could do it, there is no reason why you should not be able to achieve the same.

It was sometime in 2014 that after having worked for over 20 years in various organisations, I finally decided to take the plunge to become a freelance consultant and trainer. Little could I have foreseen that I would be authoring at least 1 book every year between my busy assignments. Today I have published 6 books with many more in the pipeline.

Interestingly, prior to writing books, I did have a few articles published in journals and newsletter. The idea of writing a book, however, never crossed my mind as the effort for writing a paper itself seemed to sap so much of my energy that I dare not even think about writing a book. This, however, changed post an article that I wrote using steps that I have outlined here in this Book. This article relating to project management proved to be a turning point for me.

Unlike the previous articles that I had written, this one seemed "painless", so to say, to produce.

That got me thinking and I started toying with the idea of writing a book using an improved version of the very same method. My journey had started. And finally the day came when I launched my first book "Mind Maps for Effective Project Management".

During my workshops and consultancy over the years as a freelancer, I have come across many people, who have expressed the ambition to pen a book. And this Book is for all those sincerely looking for answers to fulfil this desire. At the same time, I would like caution you that the focus of this Book is entirely on how to help you get your book written fast and it does not deal with other subjects such as book marketing, publishing etc. I will save that for another book. The step by step process that I present in this Book is useful for all types of non-fiction writings such as project reports, thesis, product manuals etc. Although the method can also be applied to fiction writing with a little tweaking, non-fiction writing is the focus of this Book.

Having interacted with several people across hierarchies in organisations, I am convinced that everyone is unique and has the ability to convey an equally unique message, which can be beneficial for a larger audience when expressed through writing. Your message could be a life changing gift for someone somewhere on the planet. So go forth and script yours as well as somebody else's future!

#1 STEP 1: GETTING THE BIG PICTURE RIGHT

I believe there are essentially two reasons why so many of us are not able to complete or even begin a writing project. First, it is because we are overwhelmed by the amount of writing to be done, the information to be collated from various sources and/or the ideas to be generated. Secondly and more importantly, writing (specially a book) is akin to starting a journey where many a times the destination may not be very clear, which is coupled with a fear that you may not be able to generate sufficient ideas while penning your book. You would agree with me that whenever the end goal is not very clear, we find it difficult to garner the necessary motivation to even start the project.

So how do we overcome these two challenges?

Coming to the first challenge of "writing" the words, let's do simple maths. Assuming you are writing 10 emails every day with an average 100 words in each, you create 1,000 written words every day, which translates into roughly 20,000 words a month (taking 20 working days/month). This in fact means that consciously or unconsciously, you are already writing words equivalent to a fair size book (about 120+ pages in a 6" x 4" format). So you have the necessary stamina, so to say, to produce a novel every month! What you only need is to maintain a sense of continuity and connectivity in your written word stringing them together to create your masterpiece.

That takes us to the second challenge on how do concretize our end goal of the book to keep ourselves motivated and energized throughout the journey.

This is where Step 1 of my writing technique i.e. getting big picture right, comes to your rescue.

STEP 1: Getting your big picture right

I equate writing a book to creating a living entity. In this scheme of things, the first step is to fuel the desire, next start putting the skeleton in place followed by progressively breathing life into it. This would become clear as we move forward step by step.

For now, let's focus on the first step to fuel desire to get the big picture right.

Even before you start writing a book, you need to have a certain degree of clarity on the reason for embarking on the project in the first place along with the associated questions. I find many new authors rushing into writing only to get stuck or frustrated earlier than expected as they leave many questions unanswered at the start of the project itself.

I use a technique called *Mind Mapping* to do this, and which would also come to the rescue for subsequent steps.

So a quick word about Mind Maps for those who are new to it. Mind Mapping is a simple brain friendly technique used by millions across the globe, which has proven to aid creativity, learning and memory. For making a Mind Map you:

- Start by writing the topic at the centre of the page;
- Draw thick main branches all around the central topic;
- Pen your ideas in the form of words and not sentences on the branches;
- Continue to make further sub-branches emerging from the

main branch to detail your ideas further;

- Use doodling and images whenever you get stuck and otherwise also;
- Use colors throughout to help the brain engage better with the topic at hand. You can easily manage this by using one of those multi refill pens.

Once you have identified the main branches of your Mind Map, it gives enormous freedom to your brain to generate ideas, which can be easily captured on any of the main branches. What's more, you have the option to either draw this by hand or use any of the Mind Mapping software easily available.

Mind Mapping has been found to be a very effective tool for both personal as well as work life. In fact, a survey [1] of Mind Map software users across the globe provided the following insights:

- **_Productivity increase from mind mapping_**: On an average, mind mapping software helps busy executives to become 20-30% more productive in their work.
- **_Creativity increase from mind mapping software_**: The largest percentage of respondents said it increases their creativity by 30%.
- **_Major time savings for mind mapping experts_**: Expert users of mind mapping software say it saves them an average of 7 hours per week
- **_Presenting your ideas_**: Over 78% users said that mind mapping software helps present ideas with impact to a moderate, significant or essential extent.

Though the above survey focused more on computer drawn Mind Maps using a software, based on my own experience on learning and teaching Mind Mapping, I am convinced that these results would hold true for hand drawn Mind Maps too.

Don't worry too much if you have never heard of Mind Maps before. You would be able to grasp the essentials of this concept in a matter of minutes and easily begin making one.

With this, let me introduce the first Mind Map template as given in figure 1.1, which would help you clarify the big picture of your book.

In the centre of fig 1.1, the subject is captured as "Clarifying your Book/Writing Project's Vision". There are five main branches emerging from the centre and each would answer a question with reference to your book project.

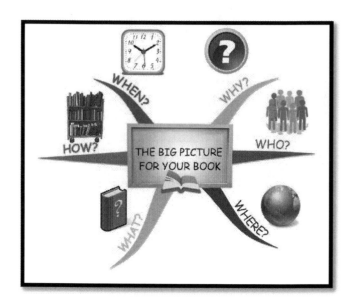

Figure 1.1: *Clarifying the big picture for your book project*

Let us go deeper into each of these questions and learn how to answer them using the Mind Map template.

a) ***So, WHY do you want to write a book?*** This is the very first question you need to answer even before writing the first word of your book. It was somewhere in 2013 that the idea of a book came to my mind. About a year later, I was planning to launch myself as a freelance trainer and consultant. I realized it was imperative for me to have a book in my name to be able to establish my credentials as a thought leader in my subject of project management and Mind Mapping). This was a core driving factor for me. In fact, there were other reasons as well: benefit a larger audience with my passion, knowledge and experience, help individuals and teams do projects better with improved project management practices, help engage teams better in projects, and of course, personal recognition with a royalty income. While building this branch, it is important that you look both from the perspective of benefits for yourself as well as what the book would offer to its readers. These various drivers for my first book "Mind Maps for Effective Project Management" [2] are captured on the "WHY" branch of the Mind Map template as shown in figure 1.2. Once you are clear about the WHY, it's time to move onto the next branch of WHAT.

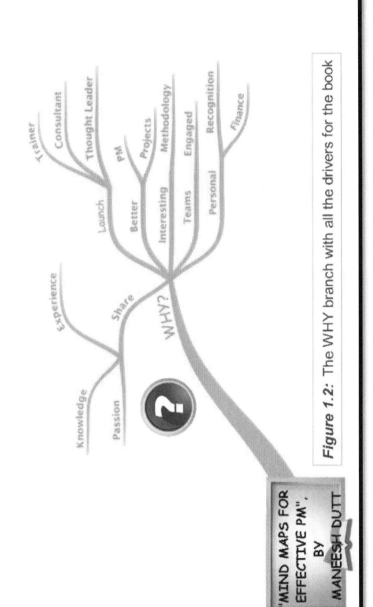

Figure 1.2: The WHY branch with all the drivers for the book

b) *WHO is the target audience for your book?* The second branch focuses on the WHO (refer Fig 1.3) wherein you identify the audience that you intend targeting. This could be in terms of age, gender, qualification, interests, job functions, geographic area or any other stratification relevant to your writing. This is an extremely important Step but many a times overlooked by new authors, or they mistakenly assume a large generic population to be their audience. Nothing can be further from the truth and you can do a quick test to understand this better. Spend a few minutes and identify what are the genre of books that you read. Looking at your genre of books that interest you, it will be easier for you to identify whether this passion to write your own book is borne of your specific occupation or interest or challenges you face or inspired by a combination of these. This would in turn give you an insight into who can be your potential audience.

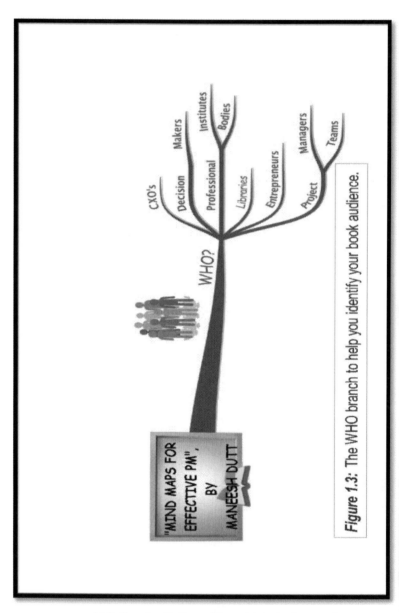

Figure 1.3: The WHO branch to help you identify your book audience.

While building the WHO branch

for my Book, I realized that besides individuals, there could be professional bodies, educational institutes or even libraries, which could be interested in such a book. This opened an entirely new market for my book, which I had not thought of before creating this Mind Map. This is an excellent example of how the brain friendly nature of Mind Maps starts triggering new and creative thoughts as soon as you begin making one.

C) *WHAT will go into your book?* The third branch "WHAT" focuses on the book structure and content. Here one lays down the top-level outline of the book by possible chapters. If you are able to additionally identify possible chapter titles at this stage itself, it would be really great, else focus on the one most important key message that you would like to convey in each chapter. A word of caution though at this stage. Do not enter into too many details as this aspect will be addressed later in this Book. You could also include special sections or additional information to be included such as figures, templates etc. In this "WHAT" section, you could optionally include the generic sections such as foreword, acknowledgement, introduction, bibliography etc. So in effect, the "WHAT" main branch helps you record the title or subject of everything that will go into your book and in the process you are able to create the first top level structure of your book. By way of an example, you can look at the "WHAT" branch for my book "Mind Maps for Effective Project Management" in Figure 1.4. It broadly captures the flow of the book --- transferred from my mind to a Mind Map. As an example of a special section, take a look at "Templates", which eventually has been the USP of this book.

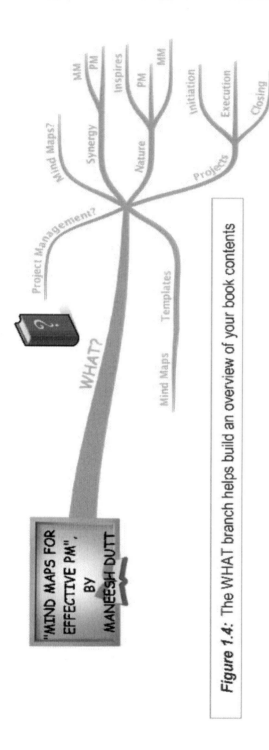

Figure 1.4: The WHAT branch helps build an overview of your book contents

c) *HOW will you publish your book?*
The next branch focuses on the "HOW" questions. So "HOW" would you get your book published: would it be self-published or would you like to scout for a publisher? What will be the preferred medium for the book: a paperback, e-book or simply a mobile-book? And "HOW" much should it be priced? In the case of my first book (reference fig 1.5), I was clear that I wanted to self-publish the book since speed was of utmost importance for me to have the book ready as an important resource for my workshops and consultancy.

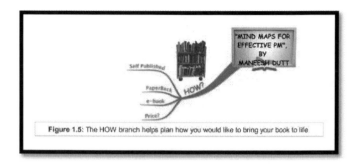

Figure 1.5: The HOW branch helps plan how you would like to bring your book to life

d) *WHEN do you plan to publish your book?* Finally, you have the very important "WHEN" to answer and here you commit to a timeline with various milestones such as completing the manuscript, getting the editing done, collecting reference information, publishing the book, setting up a publicity campaign etc. This is an extremely important branch as it will impart the required sense of urgency for completing your book project, which otherwise may continue indefinitely. An example of a WHEN branch is given in Fig 1.6.

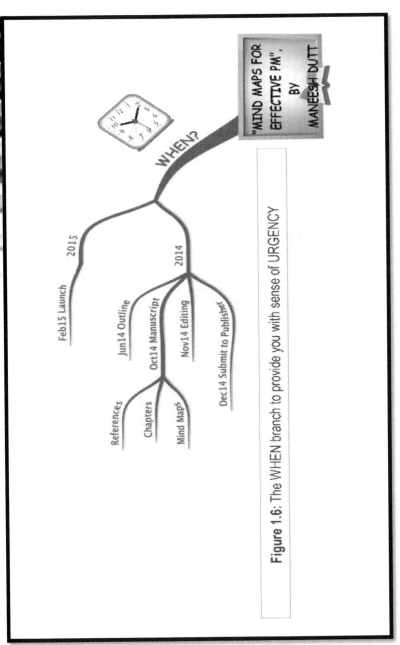

Figure 1.6: The WHEN branch to provide you with sense of URGENCY

Once you have completed working

through your Mind Map, you would have achieved a high degree of clarity about all the important aspects of the book. The final Mind Map with all the branches put together would look something like the one given in Fig 1.7. You would experience a sense of accomplishment on completing this Mind Map and feel energised to start working further on your book project. A word of caution here. If you do not revisit the Mind Map at least once a day, your motivation may not gain adequate momentum to translate into action. I would hence also recommend that you do take a printout of the Mind Map and place it where you can revisit it daily. It could be your desk, your almirah, your bathroom mirror or even as your screen wallpaper. A quick revisit would take less than a minute but it will keep you focused on your project.

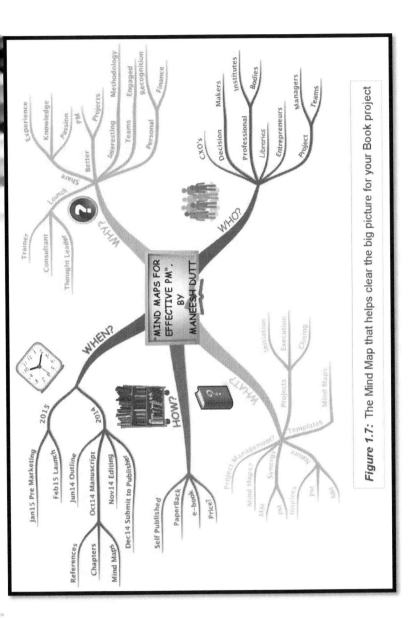

Figure 1.7: The Mind Map that helps clear the big picture for your Book project

There are three different methods through which you could build this Mind Map to gain complete clarity about your book project. Feel free to experiment with each one of them or choose one, which you like the most:

a) **Using Software Driven Mind Mapping:** This is very similar to the process that I have explained before, using a software to build your Mind Map. The template for this (i.e. Fig 1.1) is readily available with me to share with you. Just drop me an email at maneesh.dutt@outlook.com with the subject **"MM Templates for writing my book"** and I will enable access to you for the same (i.e. for all the Mind Map templates provided in this book). You will receive, via email, instructions on possible Mind Mapping software tools that you can download and start working with the provided templates. If you are already using a Mind Mapping software, it would probably take less than 5 minutes to build the template provided in Fig 1.1. You can then take a little longer to think through your complete Mind Map. Even if you have never used a Mind Mapping Software before, do not be afraid of starting to use one as most are extremely user friendly and you do get used to them quite easily.

b) *Hand drawn using a Mind Map template:* If you are new to Mind Mapping, I would recommend that you start with a few hand drawn Mind Maps before switching over to a software driven Mind Mapping. For hand drawn Mind Mapping, simply start by using an A4 size sheet in the landscape layout. Draw the Mind Map template provided in fig 1.1 on this sheet. Alternatively, with the access made available to Mind

Map templates (as highlighted above under *point a*), you could simply take a printout of the template (fig 1.1) with the main branches already drawn on it and then build the sub-branches by hand. Use colors and images throughout to trigger the creative potential of your brain.

c) **Using a Mind Map Mandala template:** A Mind Map Mandala is a new concept that I have introduced in my book "Live Life Colorfully" [3], which combines the power of Mind Mapping with the ancient art of Mandala. Mandala is a Sanskrit word that generally speaking means a circle. In common usage, Mandala is a generic term for any diagram, chart or geometric pattern that represents the cosmos metaphysically or symbolically; a microcosm of the universe. It is a symbol used in many Indian religions as an aid for focussed attention or meditation and even for creating a sacred space [4]. Figure 1.8 provides a Mind Map Mandala template equivalent to the figure 1.1 template. A Mind Map Mandala helps us bring greater focus to the subject at hand through coloring, which is known to have a calming effect on the Mind. So we begin by coloring the central big Mandala and then build our Mind Map commencing with the main branches. You will notice that there are smaller Mandala figures between the branches. Should you find yourself getting stuck at any stage, simply start coloring the smaller Mandala figures. This would allow you to again destress and engage with the creative side of your brain thereby keeping the flow. A Mind Map Mandala may take a little longer to make but it allows you to go much deeper into the subject and even lends a touch of sacredness to it. If you enjoy drawing and painting, this could be your preferred style for Mind Mapping. Access to this template (in jpeg format) will also be enabled for you (refer to instructions for access under *point a* above) and you can take a printout of the same for "drawing" the Mind Map Mandala for your book project.

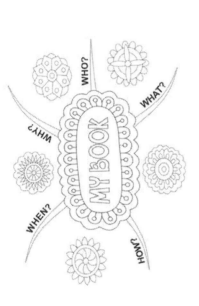

Fig 1.8: A Mind Map Mandala template for clarifying the big picture of your project.

Experiment with any one or two of the above three methods, which appeal to you. And once you have completed the Mind Map (using any of the methods), spend a little time to reflect on it. Some questions to ponder on in the context of this Mind Map are follows:

- How do I feel on completing this Mind Map? Do I have greater clarity or are there more questions to be answered?
- Does my book have sufficient "WHY" reasoning for the people to benefit from?
- If there any unanswered questions or doubts in the project, who can help me best answer these?
- What I am willing to sacrifice to complete this writing project?
- What according to me will be the biggest challenge in this

whole journey? How will I overcome it?

As mentioned earlier in the chapter, once you complete this Mind Map, you will not only gain clarity about the reasons for writing the book but would also be constrained to think about a number of activities, which go beyond writing and are essential to planning a book. Laying the foundations correctly is the first step towards producing a winning book project. Finally, do not forget to put this Mind Map in a place where you can quickly revisit it daily and create the desired motivation to devote a couple of hours regularly to your project.

With this, let us move onto the next step on your book writing project.

#2 STEP 2: PREPARING YOUR BOOK'S FRAMEWORK

Book writing is akin to any other manmade creation requiring increasing layers of clarity as we progress forward. In the previous chapter, we clarified the big picture for a better grasp of all possible aspects of our book and create sufficient hunger to take it to completion. If you have already completed the Mind Map as shown in the previous chapter, you would have realized two important things by now. One, you would now have better clarity and focus about all the activities that need to be undertaken. Two, you would have clearly identified any unresolved issues or bottlenecks that may come in the way of your book project. Both these realizations are major steps forward in your journey. And the good news is that it should have taken you less than an hour to make the Mind Map (as detailed in step 1) to reach this level of clarity.

We proceed ahead in this chapter to move onto the next step of getting the skeleton of your book ready. Your book's skeleton or framework will act as a fantastic anchor to build the storyline while maintaining clarity and focus. Let us get started with Step 2.

Developing your Story Line

While in Step 1 we had looked at all the possible aspects of the book, Step 2 focuses on elaborating the "WHAT" branch of Step 1. You would recall that in Step 1 in the "WHAT" branch we had captured the possible top level contents in terms of the chapter titles or the key messages. In Step 2, we detail this further using a Mind Map as shown in figure 2.1.

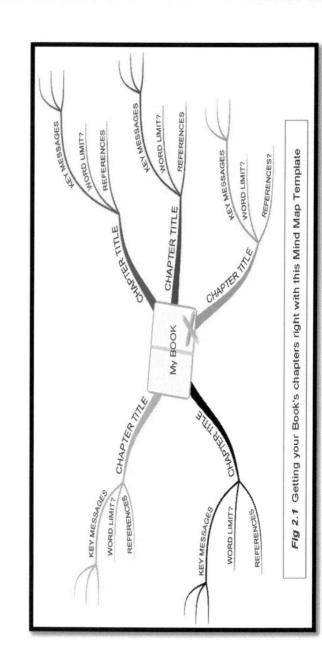

Fig 2.1 Getting your Book's chapters right with this Mind Map Template

Start by putting the proposed title of your book in the centre. Do not worry about the accuracy of the title at the moment because this may change a little with newer ideas flowing in as you progress with your book. But all the same you do need a title to anchor your book.

Next begin by writing the titles of the chapters of your proposed book on each of the main branches. Again, do not worry too much about the accuracy of the titles. The primary objective is to have placeholders, which allow your thoughts to flow. Once you are ready with the titles of the various chapters, create three child branches, viz, the first to capture the top 3 key messages that you would like convey, second to capture the approximate word length of your chapter and third for identifying any additional sources or references that you would need for your book.

At this juncture, once you have identified the chapter titles (on the main branches), feel free to move across child branches of different chapters as your thoughts arise. It is normal, say for example, while jotting key messages for chapter 1, an important key message for chapter 4 may arise in your mind. Should this or something similar happen, just capture it on the child branch of chapter 4 and then come back to your key messages for chapter 1. This is one of the biggest advantages of Mind Maps in that it provides freedom to capture all your thoughts on one or the other branches in a free-flowing manner.

You could also include in this Mind Map additional branches for elements like "Foreword", "Acknowledgements", "Dedication" etc., which would make your book complete. You may elaborate on these branches also to keep a record of important elements to include therein.

A few quick things to do once you have worked through this Mind Map. Firstly, add all the words estimate to determine the approximate word count of your book. As an example, in case it it adds up to 20,000 words, you would know that if you manage 1000 words every day, you would need just about 20 days to have the first draft manuscript ready! Of course, in reality it may take a bit a longer due to the research involved, amongst other things, but this methodology would help you have a fair idea of the effort and time required for your book.

Next, once you start with book writing (will discuss this in the next chapters), you may use this Mind Map as a dashboard to monitor progress. As an example, I take a printout of this map and as a particular chapter or main branch element gets completed, I highlight it with a colored marker. This acts as an immediate indicator of how far you have come on the way to your destination. Every new highlight gives you an adrenalin rush as you start moving to the final completion of your book.

As in Step 1, you again have the option of building your Mind Map in any of the three ways presented in the previous chapter. Should you prefer a software driven Mind Mapping, simply drop me an email at maneesh.dutt@outlook.com with the subject **"MM Templates for writing my book"** and you will get access to the template given in Fig 2.1 (along with all other templates in this book), which you can start using immediately with your preferred Mind Mapping software. Alternatively, you can hand draw the Mind Map on a blank A4 size paper. Finally, you can also use the Mind

Map Mandala approach and use colors to build your Mind Map Mandala as given in Fig 2.2 taken from my Mind Map Mandala coloring book "Live Life Colorfully" [3]. You will get access to the jpeg file for this, which you can easily print and start coloring. In this Mind Map Mandala, you need to put the title of your proposed chapters alongside the numbers and then build the sub-branches as described in Fig 2.1.

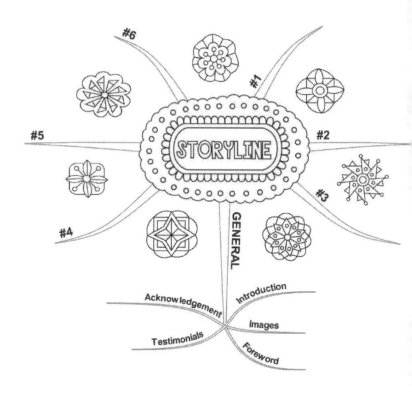

STORYLINE

#6
#5
#4
#1
#2
#3

GENERAL

Acknowledgement
Introduction
Images
Testimonials
Foreword

Figure 2.2 Developing your Storyline

At this juncture, look at your Mind Map (made using any one of the three approaches above) and reflect upon the following questions.

1. Do I feel more confident about completing my book project now?
2. Have I been able to estimate the approximate number of words for my complete book?
3. Assuming that I am spending "x" hours for writing "y" words every day, are my timelines (as identified in the previous Mind Map) in order?
4. Have I identified all the elements on the general branch?

Having completed Step 2, by now you should have much better clarity about your book project so much so that you may now be eager to jump into writing your manuscript.

But wait! Depending on the complexity of your book topic and its length, you may or may not need the next step as detailed in following chapter. Hence before you start writing, do read Step 3.

#3 STEP 3: BUILDING THE CHAPTER DETAILS

In case of book topics, which are relatively complex or books with lengthy content (say more than 50,000-60,000 words), step 3 would prove to be extremely useful to organize your thoughts better before you actually start penning your book. For shorter books with relatively less complex topics, you could directly move onto Step 4 in the next chapter. At the same time, once you have understood Step 3, you would be able to take a call yourself whether this Step is a value add for your book or not.

In the previous chapter, we identified key messages and approximate word limits for all the chapters on a single Mind Map. At this point, we build individual Mind Maps for each chapter like the one given in Fig 3.1.

In this Mind Map, the chapter title becomes the central topic along with the word limit that you have set for the chapter in the previous Mind Map made. This would again help maintain focus on the chapter topic and give you a fair idea of the amount of effort and time required for completing the chapter. The Mind Map comprises 5 main branches, three for each of the key messages and one each for the beginning and end of the chapter.

As a thumb rule, you must allocate approximately 30% of the total words planned for a chapter for beginning the chapter and for concluding the chapter. The balance 70% can them be distributed across the identified key messages forming the core of your chapter. Before beginning work on the main branches, I strongly recommended that you identify how you intend distributing words on each of the identified topics on the main branches. This again helps maintain focus and estimate the effort required for each of the branches.

The first main branch to focus on in this Mind Map is the "BEGINNING". Here jot down ideas or structure how you would like to begin the chapter. It could be a reference to the problem statement that you seek to propose a solution for, a story, which captures the essence of the chapter, or even reference to some statistical data, which reinforces the issue that you seek to tackle. Just a reminder, use only keywords or micro sentences to capture your ideas on the Mind Map branches.

In the next three branches, we build further on each of the key messages of the chapters that you had identified through the Mind Map in the last chapter. In each of the branches, you must detail further how you would like to present each of your key messages. Here you will both identify the elements required for presenting your idea to your intended audience as well as how you would like to organize them. This would be

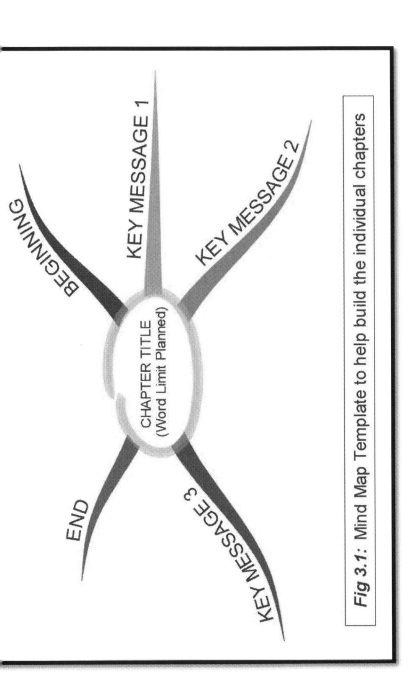

Fig 3.1: Mind Map Template to help build the individual chapters

totally unique based on your thought process. Again, for access to this template in fig 3.1 drop me an email at maneesh.dutt@outlook.com with the subject **"MM Templates for writing my book"** You will find yourself defining quite easily the sub-branches for each of the key messages through this facilitated process .

Finally, identify elements, success stories or other facts on the "END" main branch that help reinforce the message provided in the chapter. And additionally, do not forget to make a connect with the next chapter to always impart a sense of continuity to the reader.

Complete the individual Mind Maps for all the other chapters in a similar manner. On completion of the Mind Map for every chapter, do spend a little time answering the following self-reflection questions:

1. Do you have sufficient clarity to start working on your manuscript for this chapter?
2. Are any additional references required over and above those identified in the previous Mind Map template of Fig 2.1? If yes, do record these also in your Mind Map.
3. Is there consistency between the key messages planned for the chapter?
4. Would it better if any two key messages are merged into one or a key message would be better explained when split into two?

At this point now, you would be clear about the detailed structure and end point for each of the chapters and hence also your book. It would now be relatively easy to start writing the manuscript. This is exactly what we tackle in the next chapter, viz, the final step for completing your manuscript.

#4 STEP 4: GETTING STARTED WITH YOUR WRITING

In my Mind Mapping workshops, I conduct a regular exercise wherein the participants are first asked to make a Mind Map on a subject of their interest. Once complete, I ask some amongst the participants to come and give a speech on their subjects of interest referring to their Mind Map. And this comes very naturally and easily to the participants since the Mind Map has already helped them in the first place get over the difficult part of organizing their thoughts. Next I ask the participants how difficult or easy would it be for them to now write a 500 word essay on this topic. Again, I invariably find the participants agree that this too would not be difficult now compared to a situation had they been asked to write the essay directly without making a Mind Map before.

The point I am trying to make is (and you can experience this for yourself) that if at this point you have completed all the previous steps highlighted in this book, writing the final manuscript would be nothing but a natural, easy and logical culmination of your efforts.

To do this practically you need to follow a few more things.

In step two (refer fig 2.1), you would recall that you had identified the approximate word limit for each of your chapters basis which you had arrived at the number of days required for completing your manuscript. What is more important than the number of days is the amount of time daily that you have decided to dedicate for writing the manuscript. It is preferred that you "time block" the requisite time daily for your writing. It would be easier to make it a habit that will afford better efficiencies and effectiveness. So do "time block" your calendar for your writing and give it the same level of respect as you would say to a doctor's appointment. This would help you stay committed while maintaining your focus on completing your book.

Now, once you have blocked time, the very first thing to do while starting with chapter writing is to paste the corresponding chapter branch of Fig 2.1 (or detailed chapter Mind Map as in Fig 3.1) onto your word processor software. I use MS word and at the start of each chapter, I simply paste a screenshot of the corresponding Mind Map branch (or Mind Map chapter as in fig 3.1 for longer manuscripts) for my immediate and continuous reference.

Two things happen at this point of time.

First, this Mind Map will work like a magnetic compass to lend overall direction to your work. You would have perfect clarity on where to start, what key messages to be included and where to conclude by constantly referring to this Mind Map throughout the writing of your chapter.

Second, during the course of your writing, it is natural that new ideas may come to your mind. Whenever this happens, continue writing but once you are through, do spend a few moments to edit your Mind Map, if necessary, to reflect on the new scheme of things. While a Mind Map may have helped you start writing, there may be occasions when writing may trigger new ideas to be included in the Mind Map. This should not in any way undermine the importance of the chapter Mind Map that you had made. It is simply a natural process wherein new thoughts are almost always triggered whenever referring to any Mind Map. It is probably the brain friendly nature of Mind Maps that helps trigger new ideas even when you may have thought that your Mind Map was complete. It is, however, important to integrate these new ideas into the Mind Map, which would easily allow you to check for consistency with the rest of the chapters and the book.

The method that I have outlined in this Book is exactly method that I have followed to write all my books. I cannot think of any reason why this should not work for you. Still at any point should you get stuck and need help, simply drop me an email at maneesh.dutt@outlook.com. I would be more than happy to help out in whichever way I can.

With every day and hour that you invest into your manuscript, you will also grow a sense of achievement of moving closer to the completion of your book or thesis. So go ahead and don't wait for an inspiration to write your book! Inspire yourself instead to make the Mind Maps outlined in this Book, and as they say, the rest will follow!

A Final Request

I sit somewhere in India writing this book - and you the reader - could be in any part of the globe. We have made a simple connect through this book on a topic of mutual interest irrespective of our locations. As indicated earlier also in the Book, please feel free to write to me at maneesh.dutt@outlook.com for any further help that you may like in writing your manuscript.

And my final request to you is to write on Amazon a review about this book and/or your experiences and success stories in this endeavour. Your review could potentially help spread the word about this technique amongst a wider audience, and more importantly, provide me new ideas that can be incorporated into the subsequent editions of this Book.

Having invested your time reading this book, do invest a few minutes more to leave a review about it. I wish you great success in your book writing endeavour.

Additional Resources

To keep the momentum going in Mind Mapping, it is important that you refer to some of the additional resources outlined below, which can help you in your journey.

- **Access free resources available on my website**

  Many free e-learning resources have been made available on my website on the link below:

  https://maneeshdutt.com/resources/#

- **Register to Bigger Plate Website**

  BiggerPlate.com is one of the largest online repositories of Mind Maps categorised into various subjects. You can register at

  https://www.biggerplate.com

  and get inspired by all the Mind Maps accessible there. You can also contribute to the Mind

Mapping community by uploading your Mind Maps.

- **Subscribe to my You Tube channel**

  You can also subscribe to my channel (Maneesh Dutt) using the link below where I regularly post videos on Mind Mapping:

  https://www.youtube.com/chan nel/UCC-qzY7MQ0UQaNq9-iJPotA?nohtml5=False

- **Mind Mapping Success Stories**

  You can read a variety of Mind Mapping stories on my Blogsite to add to your learning at: https://maneeshdutt.com/blog/

Bibliography

[1 C. Frey, "Mind Mapping Trends Survey
]   Report 2017 available on Mind Mapping
     Software Blog pages," 2017. [Online].
     Available:
     https://mindmappingsoftwareblog.com/wp-
     content/reports/2017_MMS_Trends_Survey
     _Report.pdf. [Accessed 2019].

[2 M. Dutt, Mind Maps for Effective Project
]   Management, New Delhi: Notion Press,
     2018.

[3 M. Dutt, Live Life Colorfully, Chennai: Notion
]   Press, 2016.

[4 "Wikipedia," [Online]. Available:
]   https://en.wikipedia.org/wiki/Mandala.
     [Accessed 19 May 2016].

Other Books by the Author

Featured in "Best Book by Independent Publishers" by abcFOX and FOX34.com

If you are tired of traditional Project Management Practices, struggling with a high rate of project failures or looking for a "new", "light" and "engaging" way to manage your Projects, then this Book is for you.

How to be a good Manager? This is a question that every Project Manager needs to ask himself/herself keeping in mind his/her team and consequent project success. The brain friendly radiant thinking approach using Mind Maps can be used in projects for effective design thinking, critical thinking, complex decision making and much more. And one of the biggest benefits of Mind Mapping is that it impacts Time Management positively as it not only helps you resolve complex topics/situations faster but also dramatically improves individual plus organizational creativity.

This is probably the first book globally, which showcases the immense potential of Mind Mapping across the project life cycle from the start to finish. What is more, with every purchase you get free access to 40 Mind Map templates, which you can use immediately and benefit by applying these in your projects. A quick listing of the Mind Map templates covering various Project Management aspects included in this book is as follows:

- Developing a Project Vision
- Defining a Project Communication Plan
- Benefit versus Cost Analysis for multiple scenarios during negotiation
- Negotiation using the principles in "Getting to Yes" by Roger Fisher
- Problem Solving using 5 Wife & 1 Husband method
- Building a Customers Landscape
- Capturing Learning, Opportunities for Improvement during the project
- Time Management based on Steven Covey's Importance-Urgency matrix
- Managing Ambiguity
- Project Feasibility Analysis
- Identifying Assumptions in a Project.
- Project Benefit Analysis

- Defining a Project Charter
- Using Mind Maps to effectively apply Kano's Model
- Capturing the Project Scope
- Top level Milestone Reporting
- Delphi process for Estimating Project Cost
- Project Costing
- Skill Set Gap Analysis
- Communicating a Project Vision
- Stakeholders Communication Need Analysis
- Capturing Risks & Opportunities by Milestones
- Preparing and Conducting a Teleconference
- Effective Conflict Resolution
- Capturing and Communicating Emotions during a Project Lifecycle
- Impact Analysis of a Change to the project
- Tracking Individual Resources Activities
- Reporting and Monitoring Project Critical Path
- A "Directional" Mind Map for use as a Project Dashboard in Agile Scrum
- Quality Planning
- Cause Effect Analysis
- Investigative approach in Quality Control
- Quality Assurance via Deming's Cycle
- Risk & Opportunities Identification
- Managing Procurement
- "Make" or "Buy' Decision
- Project Pendency Checklist
- Capturing Project Learnings at closure

- Effective Retrospective Meets
- Project Portfolio Management using Mind Maps

Reviews

"Tony Buzan created a worldwide phenomenon with Mind Maps, but as with any revolutionary system that explores human thought, subsequent interpretations can often prove less insightful. Fortunately, Mind Maps for Effective Project Management by Maneesh Dutt bucks this trend to deliver an authoritative and clearly presented guide to unleashing their potential…."

- Spotlight Review, Bookviral.com

"…I highly respect Maneesh as a trainer, for setting out to help others enhance their creativity, and for taking the risk and quitting his previous job to be able to do so in the first place…"

- Chris Griffiths, Founder and CEO of OpenGenius,
the parent company of ThinkBuzan, Best-selling author,
GRASP The Solution

"… Our process-oriented industries need more creativity… so it is definitely worth investing some time to evaluate this book and its thesis for yourself!"

-Manas Fuloria, Co-founder and CEO, Nagarro

"…Maneesh has written a compelling thesis and is a must read for CXOs and project managers alike, to get the most out of projects!"

"…the initiative by Maneesh is a welcome and valuable contribution. This is especially useful for mid-level and senior people but can be used by all age groups."

Readers Reactions

"Excellent book! Was amazed to see how a seemingly simple looking 'synapses' can actually untangle tough real-life situations!"

"A must read for people who are in the business of PM and innovation."

"Most comprehensive handbook of project management"

"Very helpful book, brilliantly written"

"Fantastic book and a very valuable resource that modern project managers will find indispensable. A well-structured effort with plenty of colorful mind maps and a visually compelling marriage between project

management and the enhanced creativity mind mapping invites. A must read."

"The author has done great job articulating mind maps to apply into project management activities. Knowing majority of organizations operate as Project management enterprises, this is a great application to bring mind maps to the grassroots level in the organizations. Must read for management teams looking to enhance the quality and discipline in execution of projects."

"The book, which is precisely written, is a must read for both the compelling case it presents for Mind Maps and for the practical solutions strategy it provides."

You can also attend ***a short 1-hour online course*** based on this book on UDEMY by registering yourself at https://bit.ly/2CMPAyU

Energize your organizational meetings with the simple technique presented in this book.

Meetings, like friction, are a necessary evil for every organization. Quite commonly heard in organizations are comments like - "I love the sleep-inducing effect of our meets" or "It is surely death by meetings for us" or "We need more action and not more meetings" or "Where is the meeting headed?" or "Our meetings suck!" - and the list is endless.

Even if you hate them, you cannot escape them in an organizational set up. Imagine, however, if you could literally transform your meetings to become more engaging, energizing and effective. And that too by using simple yet powerful and proven techniques of radiant and visual thinking via Mind Maps.

Challenges exist in all organizations but many a times the top management looks entirely outside for solutions, and in the process, undermines or overlooks the creative potential of the company's internal resources. Failed internal meetings around challenges, problem solving and more, are taken as added proof by the management of the inability of their resources to solve complex problems. Nothing can be further from the truth!

Every meeting provides an opportunity to harness the unique creativity of participants as also the collective intelligence of the team. And an organization, which fails to do so is losing a golden opportunity to transform itself positively. Meetings fail or remain ineffective when individuals are unaware about simple brain friendly techniques to tap the full creative potential of the participants and this is where my Book offers to guide you.

Using the simple steps indicated in the Book backed by real life examples, you can transform your meetings around the following topics and more:

- Goals setting
- Decision making

- Communication
- Planning
- Sales & marketing
- Project management
- Innovation

The Book includes around 20 plus ready to use templates on the aforementioned topics, which you can immediately use for your meetings. And once you have learnt how to apply radiant thinking, it would be very easy for you to extend it to any area of your work. This is a ready blueprint for you to usher in positive change in your organization.

Readers Reactions

"Though this book is primarily focused on meetings, it also acts as a refresher course on the general technique of mind maps. From my 22 years of experience, I have seen corporate careers get extremely influenced by discussions and decisions that take place during meetings. By teaching you how to apply the technique of mind maps, this book will prepare you extremely well to add your value in team meetings and workplace communications...."

"Author through this book has given tool and methodology where you can use the meeting as a learning space and effectively use the time and energy of the group for an effective exploration and utilization of time."

"A unique way to generate interest and energy in meetings and avoid gaps"

"Meetings" per say is interpreted in many ways like five blinds experienced an elephant. For few, it is interesting, for some other it is boring, for few more it is essential, for a few it is even 'death' by meetings. Maneesh through this book gives new perspectives to make the meetings more productive by infusing the mind mapping methodology. The ready to use templates he has provided along with the book make this book more useful. I would recommend this book to all project managers and other professionals where most of the work gets done through meetings."

De-Stress and find life directions with this Adult coloring book with a difference.

The nature of life is such that we always face challenges either big or small. It is easy to get bogged down by problems, which in turn cloud our thinking process, making it even more difficult for us to surmount difficult situations. Would it not be wonderful if we had a tool, which could help raise our level of thinking, allow us to destress, give us the necessary motivation, and most importantly, enable solutions to emerge from within us? A Mind Map Mandala is precisely that thinking tool, which can help us in life's multiple situations. When Mind Mapping is combined with the ancient art of Mandala coloring, it becomes even more potent helping open hitherto unknown doors for us and letting us relax.

So, whether you are looking for self-help or self-improvement, this book could be your turning point.

You will discover in this Book how Mind Map Mandalas coloring can help you

* Discover your life purpose
* Achieve your life goals
* Understand and Manage your emotions to destress
* Change unwanted habits
* In Decision making
* Solve life's complex problems
* Write a book

All you need are a few color pens to get started and allow the Mind Map Mandala coloring book guide you to your destination.

Reviews

"When focusing deeply on a simple task, other anxieties become less present, less pervasive, allowing for greater clarity of thought and this is the principle that underpins Dutt's Live Life Colorfully. Readers familiar with Dutt's previous release, Mind Maps for Effective Project Management will be in no doubt as to depth and breadth of knowledge he brings to the subject and here he shares another powerful tool for turning great ideas into a functional reality."

- Spotlight Review, Bookviral.com

"Dutt's book is a beginner's guide to the potent tool that enables one to unlock his or her creative thinking prowess"

– Punya Srivastava, Associate Editor, Life Positive Magazine

Readers Reactions:

"The book is great, I just learnt so much from it. I can see outside the box, clear thinking, how to Mind Map with colorful Mandalas. Maneesh Dutt has easily explained the Mind Map techniques in a fun and relaxed way."

"A wonderful approach to unwind yourself by way of coloring and thereby overcome stress."

"A must book to read, easy to understand with deep positive impact."

"Maneesh is a vivid writer. He has created the right amalgamation of mandalas and mind mapping, helping structured thinking and pragmatic approach. A very useful tool in

decision making and a highly recommended read."

"Great book - very helpful in setting goals. Perfect Christmas gift."

Struggling to teach your child? Use the simple techniques presented in this book.

This Book is for you IF

... you are at your wits end while teaching your kids

...you believe that there must be a more creative way to teach

...you are willing to invest a little more time to learn techniques to make learning fun for your kids

...you truly believe that children are more intelligent than us

It is easy for a child to ensure laser like focus while playing or when engaged in something of his/her interest. A child does not need to learn to concentrate and focus. He is a natural at it! The real problem statement is, therefore, not how to increase a child's ability to concentrate. It is in fact how to revolutionize our teaching methodologies to match the energy and enthusiasm of a child.

This is what the Book is all about.

Reviews

"Working as compact guide, this book offers techniques which enable a child to move from a low understanding-low memory zone to a high understanding-high memory zone in the understanding-memory quadrant. Dutt's book gets my recommendation"

– **Punya Srivastava, Associate Editor, Life-Positive Magazine**.

"Maneesh presents a strong case in point to make learning enjoyable for students leveraging on the inherent strengths of a child. The Book is full of ready to use practical advice. It is a must read for both eager as well as anxious parents along with teachers, who would like to make the learning process more engaging for a child."

"Pramod Maheswari, CMD & CEO, Career Point Ltd, Chancellor, Career Point University Kota (Rajashthan) & Hamirpur (Himachal Pradesh), India"

"I first met Maneesh when he attended one of ThinkBuzan's Mind Mapping courses. Maneesh shares his experience and passion for the application of Mind Mapping in this book, and both you and your child will benefit from its teachings."

Chris Griffiths, Founder and CEO, OpenGenius, creators of the iMindMap, DropTask Tec Marina. Best-selling author, GRASP: The Solution, Penarth, Wales

"There is a dire need to make learning simple and engaging for children in this age of excess information. Mind map is an important technique to understand and combine various elements of a topic/subject. I believe Maneesh's book with his insights and practical techniques of using Mind maps will really benefit both students and teacher."

Vinay Sharma, Business head - Digital & Services, S. Chand Group, India's leading education content and services company

"Maneesh's latest release "How to Help Your Child Focus & Concentrate" opens a new door in learning and will enable students to discover their true potential using Mind Maps."

Ms. Seema Sahay, Principal, G.D. Goenka Public School

Readers Reactions:

"Mind Maps for kids is an awesome tool to help them get focused."

"Happily recommending this book to students."

"Life altering techniques in child teaching methodology"

"...I only wish if somebody taught me in this way in School."

".... the book has helped a lot, I'd say that the book will surely reach out to a bigger crowd and influence more students' minds".

"Very impressive and must buy book for young Indian parents"

"It is great reading, simple language and focus on main content rather on stories. I would highly recommend this book for parents."

"I am a student of grade tenth. ...My favorite part of this book was from the second chapter when things were told about the education system these days wherein games and other co-curricular activities are not given much importance rather than academics because these issues are hot topics of discussion among peers i.e. students. So, all said and done the book has helped a lot ..."

"...this book has really re-ignited my interest in the subject and given me a new dose of motivation to use not only Mind Maps, but the

related practical techniques presented in the book while teaching my child."

Give a Boost to creativity in your organization using Radiant Thinking

Organizational Creativity is a potent competitive advantage in any organization, but many a times not given its due importance. The journey towards becoming an innovative organization starts by sparking the creativity of the employees. Generating new ideas or overcoming challenges in an organization is easily aided using the concept of radiant and visual thinking via Mind Maps. This is a quick read e-book to bring CEO's, HR heads, Managers and all interested to speed on the basics of Mind Mapping and how it can be applied in a variety of situations inside any organization.

About the Author

Maneesh is a Chemical engineer from IIT-Delhi, India, and an MBA by qualification. He is a Tony Buzan Licensed Instructor for Mind Maps and trained by the inventor of Mind Maps himself, Mr. Tony Buzan.

He has made it his mission to take Mind Maps to all interested. He is a sought-after consultant and trainer on Mind Maps, Creativity, Innovation and Project Management. His subject is sector agnostic and as a result he has clients from across industries ranging from Pharmaceutical to Airlines to IT to Automotive etc. He loves to express himself through his writings and has a wide variety of other interests, which include project management, writing poems, Reiki healing and numerology.

He can be contacted at maneesh.dutt@outlook.com

Made in the USA
Middletown, DE
12 March 2020

86281514R00054